Past Lives

V. Joshua Adams

JACKLEG PRESS

Praise for *Past Lives*

Adams has the right combination of world-weariness and thoughtfulness to guide the reader past frustration, disappointment, and sometimes resignation into a reduced, purified space for poetry. In his poems, we can laugh at the excesses of the past while preparing to build a sadder, truer world out of the ruins to come, or at least have a laugh that "even the language of ruin gets run-down," while memories of hips (an heiress's, maybe?) and artisanal bakeries in Columbus fly by, refusing to console us. An acquired delight.

—Jordan Davis

In *Past Lives*, each line leaps to the next in glorious unpredictability, forming a latticework of surprise. In the world of V. Joshua Adams, we have competitive knitting, beer commercials, cabriolets, and mandolin players breaking ukulele players' fingers. To employ a Pavement title, Adams's poems are "slanted and enchanted": their surrealist strangeness is sometimes meditative and sometimes mercurial with acrobatic associative jumps. These are poems of wit, inquiry, and sonic vigor that examine issues of being, textuality, and the imaginative act. *Past Lives* is "swift-winged and sharp" and "darkly bright" as its sentences spin with wryness: "Even the language of ruin gets run-down," "The question filled me with dread, / which was better than nothing," and the following excerpt, from which the title *Past Lives* arises: "A lot of people have past lives they are covering up. / For example, I was once an Episcopalian." Though Adams's poems aren't overtly emotional, he extends his antennae into a range of consciousness including desire and darkness; or, to use a phrase from Mark Doty, they are a "logarithm of decay and rekindling."

—Simone Muench

It's very cool, in this present life, to be able to attest to the intellect, importance, and unsuppressable humanness of *Past Lives* from V. Joshua Adams. These poems are written with a captivating sort of rapturous flatness, situating cultural history and discourse against a backdrop of clergy, cops, and the ordinary objects of the world. I'm so drawn to the singular strangeness of the language, the phrase "Missing the Forest for the Forest" and the toast "To the end / of the end of ideas!" One poem mentions the "dangerous thing" of "imagining a future as good as the past"; here's hoping we get a future as good as *Past Lives*.

—*Natalie Shapero*

Past Lives is mysterious and alchemical, it is the seaside floating away while eating a plate of mussels in the evening and listening to the shells drop one by one into "deep yellow bowls." The speaker of these poems is sophisticated, funny, sensual, and bewildered in a way reminiscent of John Ashbery. There is something gorgeous about the way Adams's "crystal bullet eyes" aren't just taking in the world, but capturing the world in flux, each moment brimming with imaginative excess. This book reminds us that our past lives are evershifting "ghostly canopies," that glisten when we give them language.

—*Sandra Simonds*

JackLeg Press
www.jacklegpress.org

www.vjoshuaadams.com

ISBN: 978-1956907100

Library of Congress Control Number: 2023945700

Cover illustration and design: Andreas Töpfer
www.andreastoepfer.de

Author photo by Andrew Kung

Contents

III. Third Life

That which mirrors itself in language, language cannot represent.

That which expresses *itself* in language, *we* cannot express by language.

The propositions *show* the logical form of reality. They exhibit it.

—Wittgenstein

Pain always produces logic, which is very bad for you.

—Frank O'Hara

I. First Life

Circles

They sent me to school in the great forest
planted by the timber company
where each morning the chaplain
would pray to the trees. There was a river somewhere
but I was afraid to go down to it
on account of the color of the water—
menacingly clear, as though all the silt
and leaves and branches and rocks
had no real contact with anything.
Things sat or floated on, that was it,
nothing mixed. I usually couldn't find the river anyway
and was always getting lost in the woods
until the wardens came galloping on their Arabians
to bring me back for my punishment
of competitive knitting. I never won, or even made a hat
or scarf I would not be too embarrassed to wear,
and so when winter came
I was not only chastened but chilled.
That's when you found me, staring at the stopped clock,
and showed me the way out: a ritual
where we barred the door, turned up the halogen lamps,
and stared at each other until we decided
which swimsuits most flattered our blanched bodies,
high-cut one pieces or string bikinis.
The parrot helped too, from his roost in the common room,
even if he only said things he had been trained to say:
What color. Be good. Wanna go. Wanna go.

Discourse on Method

We were sitting cross-legged
on the cement in La Spezia
when you turned to me and said,
"I have forgotten why Louis XIV
revoked the Edict of Nantes."
This seemed to raise an important question,
namely, what is to be done
about French history in the present?
And by the present one did not mean
here and now, sharing a cigarette
and hoping that the train to Pisa
has air-conditioning and a restaurant car,
but here and now as in *the* here and now,
which is oddly hard to pin down,
since it always seems to be *there* and *then*—
and by French history one did not mean
just the history of the French nation
or the French-speaking peoples
but history *as such*, which is also somewhat difficult
to come by, since you can't really enter a bookstore,
even a very good one, and ask for a book like that,
a book of history as such.
What one meant was *can we do anything
about everything happening?*

The question filled me with dread,
which was better than nothing, but not by much,
so I decided to look at the beach for a while
and find the exact place where the sand became damp.
I once had a theory about beaches and infinitude
but the basis of the theory was contested
in the interim, by certain developments in my person,
including a theatrical humility.

I remembered Descartes' argument
concerning God's perfection and goodness,
that these were a sort of transcendental insurance policy
guaranteeing all our knowledge
in the event of an accident, like an accidental doubt
of God's perfection and goodness,
something that might just happen someday
like a tree limb falling through the top of an old cabriolet
and marring the sheepskin seat covers.

One could see this much was clear about La Spezia:
the environs were long on description
and short on analysis. The wine? It sufficed.
We had planned to bring some back
but the innkeeper confiscated it when he discovered
our sins against the modesty of the female form,
a misunderstanding of miniature proportions,
except that we didn't yet speak his language,
and could not adequately express,
neither as compensation nor genuine admiration,
the praise we had for the way he and his wife
had prepared our mussels earlier that evening—
supple, spiced, and sweet, we were hardly embarrassed
to moon over them as we dropped their shells,
one after another, into the deep yellow bowls
with the laughter of the sea behind us.

Nautical Maps

In the basement we queued for our tickets.
Things had been tough since the mandolin players
broke the fingers of the ukulele players.
Management had let the place go:
water rejoiced on the seams of the plaster
and the chatter of the bilge pumps
kept breaking into the lulls of our conversation.

I decided I needed to enlist, to serve my country
in the war on dessert. It's tough work, each day,
this being mostly righteous but subtle about it.
Something had stared long enough to go blind;
that's when it became a good idea to be sound.
The captain didn't know where I could make a difference.
He suggested I might try being an altar boy
but this didn't sit well with my wife.

Beaufort, South Carolina is a small, picturesque town
in my memory. A girl who lived there
was once the person I most wanted to resemble.
She had red hair, tending to pomegranate,
and there were seashells tastefully arranged
on the shelves of her living room.
Not to mention the nautical maps, painted with sailboats
full of philanthropists and the otherwise insured.
They were wearing too much plaid for my taste,
but my taste doesn't count. I haven't been on a sailboat
since the nineties, when I dropped a widget overboard
into New York Harbor, and the Coast Guard renewed an interest
in my uncle's career as a smuggler of rare birds.

This isn't meant as a cautionary tale, strictly speaking.
A lot of people have past lives they are covering up.
For example, I was once an Episcopalian.
I know, the embarrassment of it is really too much.
I went for the singing, mostly, but this is of course what everyone says.
I went for the singing, like they didn't have a choice in the matter.

Somewhere in California

in the 1960s, a young woman studying psychology
goes to see Ray Charles with a man she's recently met
and they decide to marry.
She calls her brother and his wife in Las Vegas
and her mother and father in Queens
and everyone comes on shiny DC-8s to San Francisco.
They are wed by a chaplain in an open-necked shirt
in the presence of a cousin nobody has seen since
on a rolling campus of live oak.
The windows to the chaplain's office are open.
In comes the sun and, faintly, the ocean.

The long-haired groom shakes hands
with the short-haired doctor father of the bride
and they go together to the train tracks
so the groom can record train whistles for his research.
Tape recorder on his hip, microphone aloft,
he leans toward the tracks
and the doctor father of the bride, watching, has reservations.
Afterwards they go into town
and the doctor father buys them a Volvo
and the husband and wife drive it to Texas, to the rest of their life.

All this sets it spinning:
births and deaths, divorces and marriages.
Love there until it's not
only to reappear unexpectedly
like a phone call from an old friend
who followed a man to Buenos Aires twenty-two years ago.

Tropes

Grandmother was doing her cross-fit routine.
Her dogs were in, so I played fetch
with the ugly, three-legged mix. He looked eager for a friend,
but the bastard bit hard enough to draw blood.
 "What do ye *know*, who would feign conceive,
the inner life of *beasts*?" offered the handyman,
stripping mildew from the patio furniture
with lacquer remover and an angry sponge.
Wrapping my wound in the bathroom,
I admired the photograph of the banded butterfly fish,
and the jet silkscreen of a long cigarette
whose smoke made a speech bubble that read
"All you need in life is tremendous sex drive and great ego."

I dressed for dinner at the dead man's house,
where guests clustered around the edges
of the topaz pool. Aspirational catering,
aspirational jazz trio. A couple from Memphis
had opened a dispensary, and the librarian from Waco
was tracking down setlists of his father's funk band.
Somebody won a scholarship to study meritocracy.
One therapist said to the other therapist,
"That's just his repressive moralism talking."
I was only there to exchange my life,
but each time I gave it away, it came back, stretched.

The party dissolved in a game of hide and seek
among the palms. Beside the cemetery gate,
two young women in crocheted overalls
tossed glowing hoops over the Southern Cross.

No sign of the dead man's grave, so I walked to the bodega
and bought a beer and an egg and cheese sandwich.
I never eat much at functions. They bore me.
And eating when you're bored is a dangerous thing,
like imagining a future as good as the past.

The Middle

catches up to you. It seemed always far off,
never receding exactly but never advancing either
and now here it is spread out in every direction you look,
the thought and its extension.

There are others here too, but as you learn
part of being there with them is not talking about it,
and another part is doubting that you could talk to them
even if you tried. What would you say?
It's no fun getting old? You don't feel old. Yesterday, you were young.
You wore your father's fur-lined, green suede bomber jacket
and carried a messenger bag. You made love to a Russian girl
on the rooftop of someone else's house. You laughed
at people wearing suits. Yesterday was decades ago.
Instead you say, *That's a nice lawnmower, Jim.* You say,
Don't talk with your mouth full. You say, *We can deduct the depreciation.*

Someone somewhere said it would come to this. An elder.
But the elders were always a little bit vague,
not to mention more than a little bit less formidable
than the person you believed you would become:
still full of passion for life and its mysteries,
indifferent to wealth, politically savvy,
fluent in matters artistic, attractive, etc. It's not a total wash,
except you can't drink like you once did
and you can't sleep like you once did
and you find that, worst of all, you repeat your stories.
Such as this one. You've told it before.

Of course, a lot of us have never had it so good.
The average end is farther away from the middle
than ever before. Years of slower diminishing stretch out ahead.
There will be time to solve our problems,
time to refreeze the sea ice, regrow hair, reinflate cheeks.
There will be time to read Tolstoy and Proust,
to take up painting and get serious about things
like wine. And if not, well, why not just do what the man says,
and eat and drink and live each day deep as your last?
Nobody does that, though, especially people.

Question of Tense

The window frame is not an allegory. It is a window frame. The sky fills with cheese curds and tropical fish. Did you say something about violet hands or violent hands? I didn't hear; I was breaking the mirror.

This morning the seaside floated away. The tour guides sweat and point to the listing inn, crusted with pastel umbrellas. It had that fountain you so loved: two bronze boys barehanding fish from a brook, the younger's face dark, save for an oblong upper lip rubbed to a sheen.

Thousands of tiny paper cups surrounded the cemetery. In the center of the flag there was a hole. In the center of the hole there were trees and air. For once things appeared as they are. What could it mean.

Bohemia Bagel

Even the language of ruin gets run-down.
Statues tire. The blue copper roof melts
through its gutters, and the bridges relax their arches
into the lazy water. It was not even a dream,
that country, but something we were keeping around
without much care, a vacuum cleaner in the downstairs closet,
quietly obstinate in persisting. This was hardly news,
that the serpent-peppered maps with their winged ships
buoyant as the overture of the *Zauberflöte*
offered no real territory to penetrate.
One went anyway. For the waiters, maybe,
the way they balanced delicate glasses
on ugly brown plastic trays, their studied wish
for indifference to being cast into myth. Or for the castle
filled with live raptors and dead deer. Don't tell me you've been there.
Or for the gilded art-nouveau elevator, high above the arcade,
where a dentist's assistant boarded at two and exited at five
and gave a most frankly appraising look, top to toe, widely smiling.

The birds are a problem.
It would be OK if there were only crows.
Nourished by the memory of violence, they look
almost human. We can handle them with latex
and anti-depressants. It's the others, the quick, small, and melodious,
and the big fierce swooping shadows, beloved of the dead gods.
They practically wring the word beauty from our faultless throats,
stealing the breath we were going to use
to polish our sunglasses with our shirts
and then say dishonestly, "Yes, I've read it."
Oh, for a good rifle or at least a slingshot!
But where would I buy such a thing in this neighborhood?

It's all handbags, handbags, chocolate.
Get used to gratification, say the windows with their laser-etched logos.
Gratification is here to stay. It is not going anywhere.
How embarrassing.

Someone hands me a pamphlet.
It promises we are on the cusp of a general theory
of alchemy. Soon, very soon, our tin cups
will be worth the work of a thousand afternoons
discovering avoidance. Until then, the glow
of morning's bath evaporating in the afternoon, and trams
with hundreds of strangers, each looking so familiar
he could star in the movie of your father's life—
all of these will keep us warm and clothed.
That's harder than answering the telephone
as if it's always the first time you've called.
Like tennis or chess, it's doubtful you will become a master,
but the cultivation is the thing
or at least the sound of the word *cultivation*
as you repeat it silently to yourself in the supermarket.

Views

Gull's egg shoulders peeking out,
you sip from a bottle while the dunes grow
geometric wood and glass. I turn and wave,
then stumble into muck, receive a silent laugh.
Freshwater's not for me. But your father,
in his pastel trunks, insists the Lithuanian nobles
were the last to give up their paganism.
"You know what this means," he says. I do not, but nod.

The city has everything we need but nothing we want,
so we pinball on-ramps in a tight little car,
sky and land graphite, we're drawing it ourselves,
it's drawing us, past mills, casinos, and concrete cooling towers
like the thighs of a doll face-down in the earth.
Under spotlit bookshelves of self-help
and military history, I slip under one waistband,
then another. Skyscrapers bottom into the lake.

The house sells, your father remarries a botanist,
and I write this from a cabin in the mountains
years on with my hairdresser, Dawn.
We visit hilltop mines to drink and shoot BBs and feel gravity.
We lie in the hammock and listen for colors.
She brings me to a Mexican place run by an Indian widower
who pastes icons of saints behind the register
and hangs a last supper in the dining room.

Missing the Forest for the Forest

Everything useful had been requisitioned
to suppress the rebellion in the laboratories.
Researchers were assembling readymades
out of funnels, burners, and flasks,
and nakedness like that, sometimes it's enough.
to make people pause. Police called headquarters
and asked for the chief art historian-in-residence—
there might be something to save in the décor.
The chief convened a committee formed
in the wake of the last insurrection, but the committee,
saddened by their experience with a recent restoration,
did not know if they had permission to give.

I lingered over your letters, picking stray threads of twine,
appreciating the steep angle of ink on the envelopes,
the scent of paste and raked grass. Opening one, I found
a brownish outline of a flower with its bouquet of dust,
and read *As there was a timbre of those lacquered chests*
in which the bridal dress and veil will wait,
as one might recognize, on the wall of a painting
of the artist's studio, a still life by that same artist,
merely by a dash of color and line within color and line,
so there is a quality of red that was not the red of blood or rust,
but simultaneous to each, living, unliving, in this I enclose.

I would have read this letter to the meadows and streams.
I would have read it to the confessors and confessants.
It would have been enough to wake that self
who appears sometimes as a walk-on in the film
we watch alone each night. But the dogs were beginning to bark
and, besides, you asked me to burn them all.

The buses were running, though few knew for how long,
and they were crawling with eager caricaturists.
Here, on the floor of the bakery, it was better to lie still,
covered in sugar and flour and wait for morning.

Serious Affliction

I stared into the abyss long enough
that the abyss started to look away.
"Why don't you try the surface of things?"
it asked in a voice whose silence carved up the ice.
Drinking a cider, not totally freezing,
remembering the sun had a benevolent side,
even hearing the buzz of some stunned insect
wandering about like the survivor of a wreck
surveying provisions, I, too, felt warm.
This might be it: no more waking nights
to ask what the other prisoner will do,
no more raising saviors and heroes in a city
where everyone steals and no one wants to be saved.
Others would not feel this way, but who were they?
What could be known of them but that they were not us,
and could never offer anything of ours?
There's something happening in Gstaad
between the old Texas families
that soiled the underground reservoirs.
My yacht's in dry dock. They're replacing
copper in the paint with strep, for the barnacles
to dig their own graves. Let's take yours.
It's enough the cage has room for a swing.
It's enough to feel the vibrating implicitly there,
on the threshold of the good world, between
the sunken Buddha head and plastic plants,
the tank perpetually forgotten and re-found.
It's enough to play the only game:
now you see it, now I get what I deserve.

Pillars of Wisdom

The dealer had an eye for the new style.
It started out hot, then took a detour
into the history books to cool off.
Trouble was, no one on the boat could stand
our recreation: plein air, suspenders, cigars,
everything dressed for a wedding that would be postponed.
So much territory to cover: canyon to steppe,
taiga to desert. Boys at the oasis threw dice
for my typewriter, but I only feigned sleep,
and made it to X before the ribbon went dry.
"What did you expect," said the dealer, waking up
to the wine being poured, "It's a mug's game."
Ibis god, teach me the ways of the scroll,
how to unroll instead of open and shut.
The gait of a scribe is a patient gait, it walks
to the rhythms of time, and patience is an art
of believing one will be thought to have known.
Nights he swam the gulf, guided by her torch,
until the light blew out and his body beached.
Some say she hung herself in grief.
I say she lived to write that all is water.

Januaries

"You've been miscast," said the actress.
Perhaps she was right, it was time
to give up, move to Columbus,
and start an artisanal bakery.
That sounded better than coming home nights
to wait for news of the sunken opportunity costs.
For now I spread hot sauce on my steak taco
and think of Ohio, my Ohio,
where I once took the turn of a year
sleeping on the remnant of a shattered a disco ball
brought down at midnight by a soda-jerk
with a broomstick. At breakfast she pulled up
her scrubs to show me her field hockey scars,
and when she bent down to kiss me goodbye
little shards of mirrored glass tumbled from her hair.
She still lives there, in my Ohio,
tucked into a cul-de-sac of brick mailboxes,
dreaming of life by the lake
under the yellowing ash trees.
I take the elevator down into bristling air.
Hard by the walls of the old beachfront hotel
some fool crocuses breach the strip
of Japanese garden. Ice plumps them, for now,
like mascara. There is the wind again,
sweeping through acres of empty tennis court.
There is the seatless bicycle no one yet steals.

The Weather

Tiny red eyes dot the orca figurine
and the ladybugs have all flown away
into the bathroom mirror. Their reproach is ahead and behind
as I lather a boar's hair brush
and rehearse my speech on the future of the nation.
Crossed-legged on the bed, resplendent
in nursing infant and magazine
she asks did I know so-and-so won a Tony?
The stairwell's leaning away from the wall,
but first there's the matter of the abandoned raccoon kits,
the new pea gravel, and the invasive bamboo.
We have chemicals to kill the bamboo, but it returns.
I'd like to go a day without thinking
of reading Blake in the bath, surrounded by candles,
thighs and knees poking up through the suds like gentle hills
one could climb in an afternoon to kill the autumn daylight.
So I plug in to organ and synth
and a tone pours me into the mold
of a figure prone on a bed, staring at oblongs
as they speed through blinds across the wall.
Vanguardist art? Bar graphs or charts?
Or nothing, but nothing in the plain old sense,
nothing but light moving into and through apartment blocks
built on each other like salt deposits on the shores of an inland sea?
The firemen have a nice life.
Just the sight of their stiff overalls tucked into boots
makes me flush. Let's bracket that whole business
about rare earth metals. It won't make a difference
to the pigeons or the lovers feeding them.

Autocorrect

I am waiting to be called
as a witness for the prosecution
in the trial of my upbringing. The courtroom fills up.
There is the piano teacher, neck ropy with veins,
the housekeeper who fell in the pool, the wax pâte
of the smiling headmaster. There is the coach
with his tightly curled beard and the coach
with his clean shave and sunglasses.
The priest moves somewhere in the back—
I catch sight of green and gold robes, smell his aftershave.
Kids are running around: J, with the puffy black eye
I gave him when he made fun of A,
there's A herself, grinning shyly out of a blonde halo
just like she did from the back of her father's Camaro.
College roommates in the balcony, banging on pots and pans.
There's that one girl I never called back,
and a few that I shouldn't have. Are they rolling their eyes?
Down in the front with their dogs sit my folks,
looking concerned: how dear my upbringing is to them!
And there it sits, charged and indicted, in a navy Brooks Brothers suit,
freshly coiffed, staring ahead, unapologetic,
while the lawyers cordially confer on points of procedure
and wait for the judge to exit his chambers.
Everyone's a little preoccupied so I light right the hell out of there
to get some air and find my wife. She said my upbringing
was not her concern, that she would wait for me
at the Vietnamese place, after she took in some sights.
Seems it's rained recently. The city hums, shaking off moisture,
purposeful and optimistic. People with briefcases walk briskly
through shallowing puddles and stop at street vendors
for pretzels and coffee. Schoolchildren pile off the bus
and into the park under a soaring Constable sky.
Someone's busking. Coins ruffle cash in the guitar case.

21

Everything functions as it should now,
even the newspapers, where, on the front page,
I see a story about reasonable people getting along.

II. Second Life

Ever More About

1.

At last we were safe in the woods.
The now of the blades at work

made the swaying sound of bees
overhead, attentive to husk.

Our bare feet brushed. What we held
was enough *this* to hide the trail

of our rust: furrowed by rain, open
to jonquil, here and here. Feverish beds

pleat dusk with mellow science.
They see us there cupped

round the stems at suck,
so we crawl on, praising our hands.

2.

Windshield bright,
night blinds.

Yellow shorts, white thighs,
fluorescent trails

singe themselves.
Closets ring,

proverbs carve
a desk and mime a cry.

Breathe to train
my beat to yours,

to say you
think unless.

3.

Nights on the feast of St. Bartholomew
we go down to the ruined amphitheater

and make love on the grassy proscenium.
You whisper: "The disease you get in this book

depends on your literacy." Some persimmons
roll out of my bag. We sit on stripped marble,

eat in silence, wince. A long way off
there's an apocryphal war, headless torsos

made of glass: posture of posture
holds our interest. Murmured vows

people the clover. I rise from the bed
only to find you have turned to ash.

Moonset

Easel, edged in vinyl leaf, precipitate
this flesh unblamed. Come, arrow. Come, vein.

Come slips and cleat and chains.
Come stucco, numb, suck in

what can be sewn: today, a rain
so absolute dunked marble into cloud,

& the infant piles into a neck,
wet where base meets debt.

Scattered through the hillside grove
thoughts of you evaporate,

scents in an elastic sun.
Shadows tell no time but this: canvas tents,

corrals of chain-link fence, soot,
puddles, sneakers, antennae—

these fix in eyes that spurn the day
to sweep noiseless through abandoned rooms.

Memorial

As *if* could slip
minutes under seconds,

sleep there, stripped and sweaty,
days numb to light.

What wonders:
green nebula eyes,

widows admitting no outside!
To be there again, there in dead space

embraced by no thing.
The thought calms,

swift-winged and sharp,
tangy as lamb's blood.

Dream-Work

Falling, parachutes hiss:
windgrammar is

tears salting the bridge
from reason.

Memory, green leash,
flags in the heat.

Hedges, hulls,
cray paper, wire.

Sew the dress,
golf in the olive

grove. Whatever
balcony glows

it's still always
an unfinished

room. Moonlover,
shoot to rule.

Vermilion boys
stand, palms up,

crystal bullet eyes
wide, *my, my.*

Default to Scotch.
Default to West.

The revolver's ok,
take that.

Untitled

I follow the scent
of your seashell dress
into the bed of nails.
It jiggers this skin.

Hair like weather covers
my face. Breath is the now,
need is the when,
entwining our wrists.

Under the arch,
sliver of lace:
we float on the brim,
under bottomless skies.

Stargazing

Scattered on concrete
painted like grass,
we spiral beneath

an indigo sky.
Mercury hums:
a face in the dark,

like a navel.
Your tongue
is deceptively strong

and riddles my
spine into knees.
Below the quiet

is quiet. Cold
affection. I never
you again.

Flight

Palisade maidens
hymn their summons
and blooddark maroon
the loveseat careens
over the cliffs.
On the pier,
a Bentley built
from a box,
ghosts of rich kids
passing judgments.
Beneath the bridge
I flapped waxwafer
wings & stopped
traffic for miles. She
bounced on her bed
covered in chestnuts
and enjoyed her
innocence. It's late.
Wind, purple shadows.
"Infinity," he said,
"was so immense."
This was too true.
Our bodies knew
flames laid end to end
never touch.

Lotus

Shock, midwinter sun.
Faces rise and roll:
gloaming eyebrow white
as negative's orange,
plaster moustaches,
hands. If a blueprint
lacks blueness?
Everywhere prisms, wavelengths,
pavements, cheekbones.
There are things we now know.
A woman may play
bagpipes expertly next to
a statue of Jimmy Page.
The potato pancakes taste
like cigarettes and the
cigarettes taste like artichokes
and the artichokes taste
like mild regret.
Mojave's blanket ignites.
Was that a dream in the road,
clutching the wheel, braking at
green, stopping on yellow?
We don't care
for hundreds of miles.
Ready to jump,
a seagull lands on your arm
and calls you back
into the ocean.

Drive

1.

If the riverbed could speak
to the river,
what would it say?
Stadiums bubble up
out of the oil;
their size is our shadow.
Glass walls surround
an empty room. Teardrop
fists halo rocks.

2.

The sky was not falling,
only on hinges.
Take the funicular
up to the canopy.
A man there can say
what you should have done
to your life.

After "Marie Antoinette"

First chum, then semaphore,
until at last the crosshair
grid goes dark.
Buried key, our liquid
pleas are bricked
knee-deep with hush,
the abject flush of palm
to eye says such, that trust
alone won't translate into reach.
We preach. But where,
and out of what relief?
Signs flank the pilgrim girls
in their square feet
and fork the path to pollen,
then to tree. Champagne
shadows sailed the privy walls
to scald the hair of those
who sewed your *fleur de lis*.
Spit guaranteed this loan
could not be called
until lips were currency.

Rites

Copper rose up, out of the ground
so I went to church,
put my finger in the font
and the water was stone.

Ranks of votives blinked.
I climbed up to touch
the Virgin's lips
beneath her marble aster.

Did I desire your blindness?
Hail shook the roof. In the aisles
there were shoes without laces.

The images are alive.
I stared into her glassy face.
Now put out your eyes.

The Sage

What's discipline   but desire

                      (Let labor be itself.
Only rhetoric propels

            Beauties of bad faith,
our hands and knees are blistered by an oath

to bury everything that breathes
& then to breath itself become as shoot to seed.

Ghostly canopies
border the cement lake.

    Their edges bleed
immense
             but slowly dying warmths.

North Country

Pry the dark of birch and salt,
of rut and hunger's fixity.

Scent rakes eyes to glass.
Don't touch me is the reason be.

Here, song gnaws bones. Each man
has lightning in his hand,

trucks bleed soap,
three-dollar bills say, "Be afraid."

Song, Chicago

Blood in the milk. Milk in the blood.

Stone my hair *breath-sand,*
        heart-poison plum.

Up the creekbed, up the treebed,
guns, lots. Polished

brittleness was a face.
        Thumbeye, thrust.

Sub-zero. Crows.

Blood in the milk. Milk in the blood.

Confidence Man

Twist this stippled plate of glass into the sun.
The arms around your neck abate, their grip

is wind on water. I see the silhouette
aground, a mastless ship peeling in wheat,

tar abscess where the captain's chair should be.
Usez, mais, n'abusez pas stamps along the pen;

Prokofiev was here tonight (again),
with his lieutenant's woman's lips.

"Fortune rips what future sews," he said.
The flies anesthetize themselves, seagulls

circle Styrofoam. Roman prostitutes
admire Mary, so I keep her pitted clean.

Ends

I don't have ideas, I have knives.
They're plastic. I use them to write
my name in the sand. You ask me
to sing, so I take out the gin
and pour you a glass. *To the end
of the end of ideas!* It wouldn't be bad
if you took off your clothes. I'm ready
to blink, if you're willing to gnash.
I don't have ideas, I have names.
They're plastic. Use them
to place my mouth in your hands.
Have you had enough to know how
to forget? Then put down the gin.
Press here to bend, press there to withstand.

Letter to the Corinthians

Walking alone in Chinatown
I had a true epiphany

of your ass: it was something
I could trick with my tongue

like a creed. That transparent skirt
was the glass; those velvet curtains

the dark. Light pooled on your scarlet back
while I was tasting your parts.

When I was a child I spoke
like a child. When I was a man I spoke

like a man: I called you up,
told you to come and you came.

With a Sigh

Under glass everything grew,
even the corpse.
                Want pointed out
of the oubliette into formative sun

but the way was blocked
by terrible flowers with terrible roots.
They did nothing but loom.

There was a pen, inkless, plumed.
Was it a bone, brushed with hair? Was it speaking?
I found as I gripped, it was a bird, stunned.

Onyx eyes & lips,
plug us into whatever you've run from.
Now try pinky & thumb.
To other ways the ways lead on.

III. Third Life

Dora

She came into the room
wearing a pale blue fleece robe.
I took it off and blue went everywhere:
into the figurine of the Virgin on the bookshelf,
the potted pansies on the porch across the street.
The white sheets in the mid-morning sun
were glazed near blue themselves.
Veins braced ankle and wrist, reaching up from under breasts,
shoulders, clavicles, up from under glassy skin,
the whole scaffold on display.

I had been reading "The Sea and the Mirror"
while waiting for her to decide what to do with me.
The first question she asked was, "Who reads Auden anymore?"
Her chest and neck were warm
but her hair, still wet, threw off a chill.
I picked up ripeness under synthetic and went to it.
Holding her hips, I thought
was she an heiress? Had she run away to avoid marriage
to a sensitive, but boring, athletic type?
Were we inside of a novel, and, if so,
was I a character or merely the narrator?

At the concert last night
a boy in the crowd kept shouting "Omaha! Omaha!"
I could have killed him or kissed him, you pick.
Dora had a sophisticate's take
on the Israeli-Palestinian conflict, on Kashmiri food, on modeling
and not modeling, on things I cannot remember
except for her mastery. "Munich is clean like a cage."
Fingers rake hair and grip.
The second question she asked was my name.

Revisionary Ratios

There's a cost to this life, I'll tally it up
said the scrap-meat, said the newsprint.

Carp come quick now, tricked now, pricked now.
Why should I pay for your *bahn-dage*, your *mah-ssage*?

Lace thigh-high and only so, oh Jesus-H, Viola,
you kid me with your pluck!

Flat lakes we go down in each night,
our lawns, sirs, shall outlive us.

My empire-builder chugs: *pa-thump*.
Those dying generations don't die quick enough.

Pilgrim

Orchids scored the doorframe. A coral face
surfaced from the foam of muffled talk,
blinked slowly in surprise, floated aside.

Letters piled on the dining table
in a blue reclining script, specimens at a dig.
"It's all there," said the man, and walked away

only to return holding a wooden top
in the shape of a ballerina, with the head
of a Pharaoh hound. The Tour was on.

"Ces journalistes me gênent," said the woman,
"They chew up all the air and then they spit."
Plastic water lilies were harrowing the pool.

From the tower in the garden, I could see the cemetery:
alabaster throats swallowed midday sun,
cats sprawling on the curbs, cut flowers begging to be pressed.

for H.M.

Another Country (I)

Turns out O's engaged to a German
aristocrat. Two miles
through the dark pretending to be interested
in Arthur Symons for *this*?
There's something wet in my Kenneth Coles.
I'll have that bottle yes.

She wants the cashmere poncho back
from her ex, C, which is why, I guess,
all seven of us are sitting on his bed,
the only furniture in here besides a pasteboard
paper-covered desk and the hard case
of a guitar. There's a Bosch Last Judgment
on the wall. That's guts. No pleaser, this C.
It rankles O enough for her to rub her thighs
against his. A whispy boy with a whispy beard
but calm and firm as his rows of Loebs,
the marked-up copy of *Clarel*.

Two girls swirled in one another's laps
argue about monarchy.
One of the designer boys looks for me
from far beneath his lenses,
touches my hand and says
"I'm amazed to hear someone speak
so honestly."

Now canker sore takes root in-cheek.
Eye sockets sink. Another blister leaks.
Didn't care and don't.
Didn't care and won't.
Never will it be again so darkly bright as this.

Paris Poem

Form is a fetish, but it's a sin to live as if. In my twenty-sixth year, I became a believer in private property, or private property became a believer in me.

Wax melts in a dark room. We have learned to love sovereignty once again, Victoria! Now show us your stuffed squirrels playing cards in a glass case.

Let me drink it off, this fin-de-fin-de-siècle. All the systematic theology in the world won't put this night back together. Great underwater lung, breathe. I swim through canyons, your bra-strap my lifeboat. Ballerinas bicycle the shore.

The coach was not, in fact, a ghost of your late father. There were boys from Kenosha popping champagne. Wind blows, up comes the dust. Asleep we were hunters, and on waking we knew it was true.

Come What May

When you meet the Angel of Death
it is a Tuesday, the air warm and wet
with the smell of turmeric and chive. Churches are closed
but cafes are open, people are sitting in sun
drinking frappés and beers.
The Angel of Death comes up beside you
as you are walking to meet your sister and her children
or as you are walking to meet your friend and her lover.
You know it is the Angel of Death
by the lightness of the hand as it touches your shoulder,
the distance of the voice that begs pardon,
the whiteness of the teeth and the orderly silver hair.
The Angel of Death asks you for directions
to the place you are already going,
and falls into step quietly beside you for a time,
remarking on how the street has changed,
the unpleasantness of the heat.

Frustrating, not to let on that you know,
but it is necessary for hope that you do so.
So instead you ask a few polite questions
such as "How long have you been visiting our city?"
Where are you staying? Will you remain long?"
to which the voice gives decorous, vague replies.
Now you are sweating a bit in the heat and the scents,
and also chilled with death-thoughts,
hopscotching through things you did and did not do.
Learning the trombone. Traveling to Africa to photograph
people taking photographs. Falling for someone wrong the right way.
You arrive at your destination. There is your sister and her children.

She looks tired as ivy on a fountain. There is your friend and her
    lover.
What is it like, waking to each other now?
A hand on your shoulder again, light as a dried leaf.
The Angel of Death says, "Thank you for guiding me," and walks
    away.

Routine

Morning, midsummer. Asphalt exhales
a white coat, skirt, and thick shoes
dappled red.

       Nights, she's a nurse;
days, she sleeps on an overstuffed couch.
Foxhunt prints stand guard.

High in the attic, a boy reads the *Odyssey*.
Souls drink blood from troughs
and speak clouds of pink mist. Embracers tumble.

Across the river in the sick city
people sicken and die. Down by the pool
the sun shines, and the gardeners break for lunch.

Death by Wild Animals Is Introduced

Katydids thick as fists
lunge half-forward in their treaty song.
The documents are wet, again;
windows shutter dampness in.

A flower stand along the road
sells maps and compasses in pots.
Smoke rises now at every longitude,
and the same words push all the tubes at once.

Let's sit. There's lobster, London Broil, beer
and rage about the sanity
of prophets and the right to sue.
Enough frivolity becomes us.

Islands

Clapboard and salt, sweetness of gas
fish mildew and rose.
Everyone's dressed for a jog
and on a brick driveway inlaid with grass
a shiny black jeep gets waxed.

Next to some pulp in the rented house
I find Orwell's essays
overdue by forty-seven years
from a public library in San Antonio.
Verse complies, he says, but not honest prose.

Every man is a part of the main.
Genuflecting into screens, killing Pinot gris,
they shout, "Build it somewhere else!"
(Never anywhere too close.)

Another Country (II)

In the elevator, in the Texas resto
on Queen St., they play all the hits
of nineteen ninety-four.

Need: *no art without passion.* Need:
permanent revolt.

      Narcissistic,
fastidious, self-doubt
can't not, it's in
         it's in the *will.*

Breakdance, blowtorch,
         burning sensation.

Unhelmet the tone now.
         Exchange is the mode,
      our fold.

No outside, but we
         can still be
happy
   as a rub and tug.

            Clever chicken wrap,
that fantastic pink,
   came from the sink, love.

Kitsch-Value

The horses sleep in luxury stalls.
We roll past subdivided mansions and loud domestic cars
while a man in a nightshirt whispers "dope"
to the swaying foam of his plastic cup.
Gaslights flick and buzz. On the reddish frieze,
the boxer's cracked coconut face leaks.
Me neat, you rocks, we skim a flotsam
of bowties, broad-brims, tattoos, and chains.
You start in about Welles, whose stolen fire
rekindles art with news of its own death.
I saw *Citizen Kane* propped up on pillows
in a school library tragically smeared with primary colors.
The opera clap made my balls retract.
But now the scene's a joke on repeat,
just like us, arguing about aura, ordering another round,
flanked by flat Ionic columns painted gold.

Triumph means killing what you love.
Feet free of the stool, I spin like a sulking kid
in an office chair, and from a mass
hunched over icons in the neon gloom, she stands erect
in fire-engine red. There's a beer commercial now,
then one for decorating dirt with shiny trucks.
She tugs it down, the mini-dress,
but with each tug the other side climbs up,
toward the carmine cataract poured down her back.
Faces whirl as she discerns the shine of colliding bodies.

You're on to *Chimes at Midnight* now, the purity of Falstaff's heart.
I reach for the smooth ground of your delicate shoulder
—early one New Year's, smoking on a frozen porch,
city of millions silent under purple snow, your borrowed parka
     barely fit—
but you only lift a glass and say, "I shall be sent for soon."

Aria for the Watchers

If I could just
stay on this bus
'til the end of the street
end of the day of the week
end of the need
for the shape of the seem
Could if I could
bus the street clean
could need the end meek
could stay the day just
'til the end of the days
(of the weeks)
'til the I of the end
(of the seem)
'til the 'til, 'til the stay, 'til the week
'til the day, 'til the shape, 'til the if

Could make the bus go
over all roads,
could touch the driver
could sit on his knee
rip the seats free
flip the railing
roll metal and flesh
baste asphalt with oil
and oil with blood
all roads could touch
all drivers could flesh
all blood could flip
over asphalt and knees
over days, over weeks
could oil, could touch
could French the driver

could jerk metal clean

Is it me. Do you hear.
Not looking, for you. They're listening,
here. Each key is a flare, a beacon,
a bee. Nowhere over true.
Bus is a plaque, buffer is you.
It is me? Your name, here. I am looking.
For you. The alphabet hides.
Each letter jumps out of a plane, of a tree,
nowhere under new.

Oh asphalt and oil!
And metal and flesh!
And day and if!
Oh shape and seem!
And blame and clutch!
And jerk and weak!
No other true!

It's time (it's been time)
to just the could clean
to meek the 'til I
to stay the stay
to if to could to
end to need bus

Imagined Community

1.

Lacy, leafless Chinese elms
canopy a man in brown.

Public housing trailers peel
but the home for sex offenders

has fresh paint on its pickets.
Up and down the sidewalk

women pick up trash in sweats,
faces older than their limbs suggest.

A couple parks, and watches them
from a lipstick eighties Coup de Ville.

The *Hamlet* overture ties us
to its gloomy strings, while, to front

a shiny pair of chrome nuts
dangles from a pickup.

2.

Bruise parka, fleece aqua:

Persian doll-face kittens dance
over greys and pinks

made where by whom from what

smashed noses short
(but not too short).

Exhaust rattles the heat-shield & blanches the crabgrass.

        Chain-link
moats the school. Children file, one finger to their lips,
another in the air.
                what skies await, what seas

Bloodshot, wind-blind, blacktop soaks
        a cracked rubber sole
to the cardboard underfoot.

3.

Change the radio. Enough Tchaikovsky.

Sonorous voice: *Much of Aleppo has been leveled.*
Sonorous voice: *The civilians were being driven to the countryside*
        but the buses were shelled.

Clatter of accent, pitch. Civilians on the radio now,
men and women shouting, slicing up static.
Bombed-out hospitals. Limp bodies.

Change the radio. Enough civilians.
"Forget the hearse, cause I never die." *Yes.*

4.

The tetrahedron is a mega church.
Outside, the sign says HAVE A BLESS DAY
every day, to the brownfields, dueling car washes,

& blinking Payday lenders.

A broad avenue drops sidewalks to ditches.

      Past the old ice tower flaking stone
a white stretch
pulls a horse trailer.

At home there are checks, paperwork, dishes.
Cardboard boxes full of unused toys.
A letter from Iceland describing the minimum criteria.
A stack of *Victorian Living*
piles on *An Intimate History of Humanity.*

Twenty Sixteen

The creek bed divides
        a riot of pinks
& fisherman's boots
plough dust to a patch of scrub

where clay pigeons fission
            through silver maples
planted to celebrate armistice.
Shotgun stock bucks labrum up:

I miss, but love the scent,
        almost nourishment.
Light as a paperweight,
or a wooden racquet

loosely gripped, the Luger flips
        a presbyter handbell peal
as each bullet heads to disc.
Sound says good,

you're good at this. Who isn't
        or couldn't be?
That's the trick, the story we know
without knowing we know it.

At last, the old Soviet machine.
        Large and long, grim
ammunition tapered sharp
for penetrating bushes, walls, and doors,

odd to aim, one always saw it
        slung mid-hip
by actors playing darker men.
But hoisted, sighted, trigger pulled,

current snaking spine
        and gut, one cartridge
vaults away, the next one volunteers—
nothing desperate or wrong

just force orchestrating air:
        like a major chord
pricks each tender scalp
in the stadium at once.

Period Piece

You hear strange sounds walking barefoot
down the middle of the street,
wearing an unbuttoned tuxedo shirt
and holding your Oxfords.
Of course, there's the familiar: medievalism
and truancy, tourism and psychoanalysis.
But there are also sounds one does not quite expect:
children, for example, waking in cars,
muzzled dogs pawing one another.
Sounds of meter maids running through *Cymbeline*
on their lunch break, or a fork clattering
on a dish at a cafe near Wenceslas square,
though you are a long way from Prague, this being Cleveland.

One autumn day, you looked over your shoulder:
the oxen were literally lowing.
Our friends are tight for the counter-revolution,
but that class is full. It's all right. I have it on no authority
that the professor is a disgraced minor functionary
of the old regime, put there to watch
the rigid commit, and to serve the state
by evaluating in its idiom. What are your options?
Impressment? Philanthropy?
Three-point perspective was good
while it lasted. Now all it does is call the police
and, wearing their hats, the police come too soon.

The Way Out Is the Way Through

It's dawning now, in the green afternoon light,
you've been mistaken for someone else.
Look around: the street is empty and silent,
houses in their motley of potted flowers and hanging ferns
salute each other like old veterans.
A lizard scrambles the tile of a Juliet balcony
under *trompe l'oeil* blue. Nobody's fooled.
There's no confetti, no photo-op, no book signing.
There will be no calls to the radio shows,
no disarming the hosts with unpretentious banter.
Obviously schools, street signs, and plaques
are out of the question, since there will be no scandal
followed by a sufficiently contrite interview
with a tough but tender anchorwoman,
the one who wrote the book about being raised by nuns.
Hardest to accept will be the lack
of encomia by rivals, delivered grudgingly
to their biographers long after your death.
Most days you just ask unanswerable questions
to audiences too streetwise to believe
there are no answers. And when you are not doing this,
you are peeling ginger or dusting the bookshelves,
or washing the household underwear.
Or taking mountains of boggy cardboard
out to the sticky bins. There, on the ground, you find
the wonderfully spherical nest, with one small, sandy egg
still inside. How long can it last—no, it's already gone.
Nothing of yours remains either, unless
someone catches here something of themselves,
lingers long enough, and, before moving on
and forgetting it for good, as you will,
thinks it might be better this way,
to be no one worth knowing.

Acknowledgments

This manuscript began in a past life. I am grateful to the many friends and poets who read my work and offered comments and encouragement. Particular thanks to the members of Sublimity City; to Sandra Simonds, for helping me get the book into its current form; to Simone Muench, for choosing it for JackLeg Press; to Jordan Davis and Natalie Shapero for their kind words; to Andreas Töpfer for a killer cover; and to Jennifer Harris, for bringing it into the world. I dedicate these poems to the *hypocrite lecteur*.

Some of the work here first appeared in a chapbook, *Cold Affections* (Plan B Press, 2018). I also thank the editors of the following journals for publishing individual poems from *Past Lives*:

Allium: "Serious Affliction"
Annulet: "Missing the Forest for the Forest"
Argo: "Letter to the Corinthians"
Ariadne: "The Way Out Is the Way Through"
Bennington Review, "Januaries"
Cathexis Northwest: "Islands"
Cloudbank: "The Middle"
Colloquium: "Period Piece," "Aria for the Watchers," "Ever More About," "Routine"
Funicular: "Imagined Community"
Jet Fuel Review: "Moonset"
Miracle Monocle: "Paris Poem," "Question of Tense"
Mud Season Review: "Twenty Sixteen"
Painted Bride Quarterly: "Bohemia Bagel"
Posit: "Another Country (II)," "Circles," "Song, Chicago," "Revisionary Ratios"

Reed Magazine: "Come What May"
Trampset: "Autocorrect"
Typishly: "Kitsch-Value"
Tupelo Quarterly: "Ends," "Dream-Work"
Variant Literature: "Views"

About the Author

Photo by Andrew Kung

V. Joshua Adams is a poet, critic, translator, and scholar. He teaches at the University of Louisville. *Past Lives* is his first full-length book of poems; a critical book, *Skepticism and Impersonality in Modern Poetry: Literary Experiments with Philosophical Problems*, is forthcoming from Bloomsbury.

JACKLEG PRESS

V. Joshua Adams, Scott Shibuya Brown, Michael Chin, Chloe Clark, Brian Rivka Clifton, Brittney Corrigan, Jessica Cuello, Barbara Cully, Alison Cundiff, Neil de la Flor, Suzanne Frischkorn, Victoria Garza, Reginald Gibbons, Joachim Glage, Caroline Goodwin, Kathryn Kruse, Brigitte Lewis, Jenny Magnus, D.K. McCutchen, Jean McGarry, Rita Mookerjee, Mamie Morgan, Alexis Orgera, Karen Rigby, Jo Salas, Maureen Seaton, Kristine Snodgrass, Cornelia Maude Spelman, Peter Stenson, Melissa Studdard, Curious Theatre, Gemini Wahhaj, Megan Weiler, Cassandra Whitaker, David Wesley Williams

jacklegpress.org

www.ingramcontent.com/pod-product-compliance
Lightning Source LLC
Chambersburg PA
CBHW031249120626
46545CB00007B/2723